WHERE WE GATHER

WE GATHER AT A SIKH GURDWARA

A Place in Our Community

by Jasneet Kaur

PEBBLE
a capstone imprint

Published by Pebble, an imprint of Capstone
1710 Roe Crest Drive, North Mankato, Minnesota 56003
capstonepub.com

Library of Congress Cataloging-in-Publication Data
Names: Kaur, Jasneet, author.
Title: We gather at a Sikh gurdwara : a place in our community / by Jasneet Kaur.
Description: North Mankato, Minnesota : Pebble, [2026] | Series: Where we gather | Includes bibliographical references and index. | Audience: Ages 5-8 | Audience: Grades 2-3 | Summary: "People who practice the Sikh religion worship in a gurdwara. The word means "door to the Guru." The Gurus were important religious leaders. Anyone can come inside a gurdwara, regardless of their religion. Sikhs believe that everyone is equal. An activity is included to help kids extend their learning"— Provided by publisher.
Identifiers: LCCN 2024054911 (print) | LCCN 2024054912 (ebook) | ISBN 9798875223242 (hardcover) | ISBN 9798875223198 (paperback) | ISBN 9798875223204 (pdf) | ISBN 9798875223211 (epub) | ISBN 9798875223228 (kindle edition)
Subjects: LCSH: Sikhism—Customs and practices—Juvenile literature.
Classification: LCC BL2018 .K2743 2026 (print) | LCC BL2018 (ebook) | DDC 294.6/35—dc23/eng/20250113
LC record available at https://lccn.loc.gov/2024054911
LC ebook record available at https://lccn.loc.gov/2024054912

Editorial Credits
Designer: Sarah Bennett; Media Researchers: Jo Miller and Svetlana Zhurkin; Production Specialist: Tori Abraham

Image Credits
Alamy: Boris Roessler/dpa picture alliance, 14, Paul Doyle, 5, World Religions Photo Library, 18; Getty Images: Dinodia Photo, 17, Lisa Maree Williams, 11; Shutterstock: Abie Davies, 12, arindambanerjee, 19, Design_house01, 20, Falak0001, 13, HeadSpinPhoto, 7, kizuuuneko, design element (throughout), OlegD, 4, Ritu Manoj Jethani, 15, saiko3p, cover, Sorbis, 10, Sumit Saraswat, 16, travelarium.ph, 9, YURY TARANIK, 8, Zixia, 6

Printed and bound in China. 6274

Table of Contents

Words in **bold** are in the glossary.

What Is a Gurdwara?

Sikhism is a religion. People who practice it are called Sikhs. They worship in a gurdwara. This word means "door to the **Guru**" or "Guru's court." There were 10 Gurus. They led the Sikh people.

There are around 26 million Sikhs around the world.

The orange flag is called Nishan Sahib.

You can spot a gurdwara from far away. Each has a triangle-shaped flag with a dark blue **Khanda** symbol.

Step Inside

Sikhs cover their heads before entering the gurdwara. They also take off their shoes in the jora ghar, or shoe house.

Removing shoes is a sign of respect.

Some jora ghar have a sink for handwashing. In India, most gurdwaras have a place for people to wash their feet too.

People wash their feet before entering the Golden Temple in India.

Water purifies the body and the mind. Many gurdwaras in India have a sarovar. This is a square or rectangular pool full of **sacred** water.

The Golden Temple in India is surrounded by water.

The water in some sarovars is believed to have healing properties.

Steps lead into the water. Sikhs will often use it to bathe before entering the gurdwara.

The Diwaan Hall is a place to pray.

The first room in a gurdwara is called the Diwaan Hall. A covered throne is at the far end. The Sikh holy book sits on the throne. The holy book is called Sri Guru Granth Sahib Ji.

The holy book is treated like royalty. It is draped with **rumaalas**. A special volunteer holds a fan called a chaur. The volunteer waves it over Sri Guru Granth Sahib Ji. This is a sign of respect.

The chaur is often made from yak hair.

Kirtan means “singing the praises of God.”

Any **initiated** Sikh can read from Sri Guru Granth Sahib Ji. They gather in the Diwaan Hall to listen to **Kirtan**. They pray. They also celebrate special occasions.

Anywhere with Sri Guru Granth Sahib Ji present can be a gurdwara.

Anyone can come to a gurdwara. It does not matter if they practice a different religion. Sikhs believe everyone is equal. Everyone sits on the floor together.

After the Services

Sri Guru Granth Sahib Ji has a special resting place in the gurdwara. It is called the sukhaasan. After prayers are over for the day, volunteers carry the holy book to this special room.

Sri Guru Granth Sahib Ji is put away at night.

The people who care for Sri Guru Granth Sahib Ji are either volunteers or work at the gurdwara.

In the morning, it is moved back to the throne. This **ritual** is called prakash.

All gurdwaras have space called a Langar Hall. It is a place for preparing and eating meals. Sikhs believe in selfless service, or seva. Making and giving out food is part of that service.

Preparing meals for others is a huge part of the Sikh religion.

Volunteers of all ages come together to prepare a vegetarian meal in the Langar Hall. Everyone eats together on the floor.

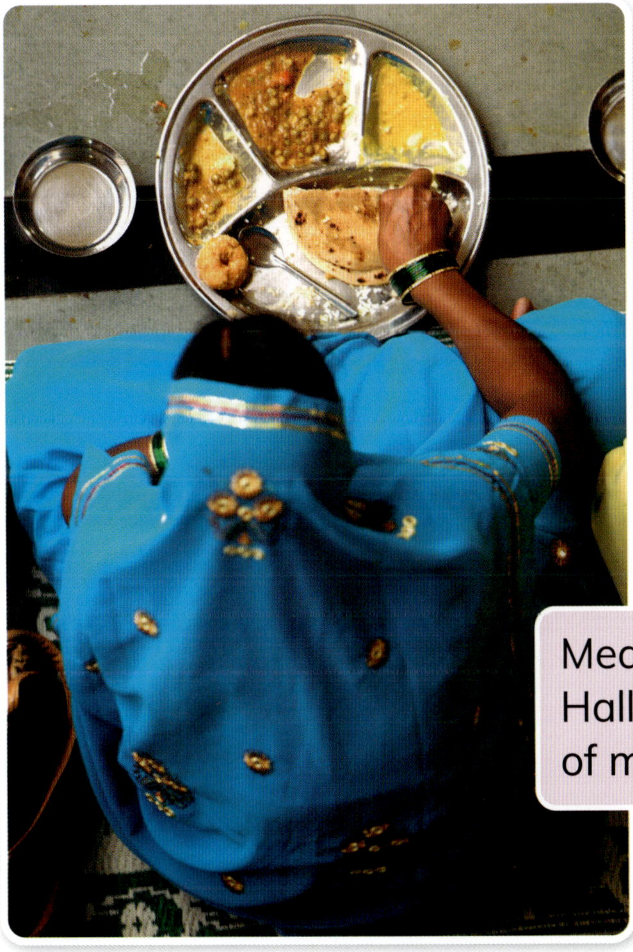

Meals in the Langar Hall are always free of meat and eggs.

Events at the Gurdwara

People visit gurdwaras for major life events, holidays, and other reasons. Many gurdwaras have classrooms for Khalsa School. Children learn about their religion, history, and language.

Students learn how to speak Punjabi at their gurdwara.

Sikhs celebrate kindness no matter where they are.

Sometimes people need help. They can find support at the gurdwara. Community members can go there to seek friendship. The gurdwara has something for everyone!

Make a Rumaala Design

Rumaala is a special cloth. It is used to cover Sri Guru Granth Sahib Ji. You can make your own Rumaala design on paper.

What You Need

- brightly colored construction paper sheets
- scissors
- glue
- glitter glue or glitter

What You Do

1. Choose one sheet of construction paper to be the rumaala.
2. Cut out shapes from the other sheets of paper. Leaves, flowers, circles, or squares are only a few ideas! Layer shapes and use multiple colors to make your print bright and fun.
3. Glue the shapes to the rumaala.
4. Add glitter, if desired. Let your rumaala dry completely before finding a special place to keep it.

Glossary

Guru (GOO-roo)—a spiritual teacher

initiated (i-NI-she-ayt-ed)—to have taken part in a process that allows someone to be a member

Khanda (KHAN-duh)—a sword with two edges

Kirtan (KEER-thuhn)—special hymns sung from Guru Granth Sahib Ji

ritual (RICH-oo-uhl)—an action that is always performed in the same way

rumaala (roo-MAH-luh)—fabric with sewn-on designs often done with gold and silver thread

sacred (SAY-krid)—holy or deserving great respect

Read More

Kaur, Jasneet. *Sikh Festivals and Traditions*. North Mankato, MN: Capstone, 2025.

Rose, Simon. *Harmandir Sahib Sikh Temple*. New York: Lightbox, 2022.

Srinivasan, Radhika. *India*. New York: Cavendish Square Publishing, 2022.

Internet Sites

BBC: What is Sikhism?
bbc.co.uk/bitesize/articles/zkjpkmn

Kiddle: Sikhism Facts for Kids
kids.kiddle.co/Sikhism

Little Sikhs
littlesikhs.com

Index

About the Author

Jasneet Kaur is the author of *Dream Big, Little Kaur* and *Dream Big, Little Singh*. These children's books highlight various personalities from Sikh history. She is also the founder of a web-based platform for young Sikhs called Curious Khalsa. Jasneet is a mother of two young Kaurs who continue to inspire her. In her spare time, she loves listening to music, creating art, reading books, and visiting various local libraries for continued inspiration.